BBC MUSIC GUIDES

BEETHOVEN PIAN

BBC MUSIC GUIDES

General Editors: GERALD ABRAHAM & LIONEL SALTER

BBC MUSIC GUIDES

BEETHOVEN PIANO SONATAS

DENIS MATTHEWS

BRITISH BROADCASTING CORPORATION

Published by the British Broadcasting Corporation
35 Marylebone High Street, London W1M 4AA
ISBN: 0 563 07304 7

First published 1967
Reprinted 1969, 1973
© Denis Matthews 1967

Printed in England by Billing & Sons Limited
Guildford and London

INTRODUCTION

The well-worn tag about the old and new testaments of keyboard music still holds. It would be a poor music library that lacked Bach's *Well-tempered Clavier* and the thirty-two piano sonatas of Beethoven. They both do far more than enrich the repertoire of an already well-endowed instrument: they illustrate to perfection the almost infinite resource and flexibility of a chosen musical form in the hands of a composer of genius. No two of Bach's fugues are alike in character or treatment. The treatment is determined by the character and the ideas, and the individuality underlined, not hampered, by the sharing of certain basic procedures. As with Bach, so, in a different sphere, with Beethoven. Think for a moment of the variety of the sonatas and the width of their appeal. Even the most casual of music-lovers has been known to succumb to the strange, veiled potency of the first movement of the so-called *Moonlight*. Is there a general-practising virtuoso who escapes carrying either the *Waldstein* or the *Appassionata* in his repertoire? (And what companion works could be more different in their affirmation of major and minor keys than these two?) The intellectual who confesses, to his loss, that middle-period Beethoven has nothing new to say to him will still turn to the *Hammerklavier* as one of the stiffest challenges for player and listener alike; yet for those who fight shy of the epic, titanic Beethoven there are sonatas in all periods that converse in intimate domestic tones. Even the youngest pianists can still find an entrance to Beethoven's world through the sonatas. As they mature in mind and fingers they may set their sights on the lofty pinnacles of the late works; but they will be constantly surprised at the unsuspected richnesses of the earlier slow movements. 'Early', however, needs some qualification in Beethoven's case. He wrote three childhood sonatas in his Bonn days which are prophetic, maybe, but are not normally accepted into the self-approved canon. Beethoven was twenty-five when he confirmed his readiness by publishing works with opus-numbers, a late starter by Mozartean standards.

From this time on, the piano sonatas have the value and the

5

fascination of being spread more or less evenly over Beethoven's creative life: they epitomize the immense journey, musical and spiritual, that this life encompassed; they illustrate the growing power of the piano itself, from rivalry of the harpsichord to unchallenged supremacy as a solo instrument; and they cover a short but vital area of history in which social changes were reflected in the worlds of all the arts. It has been said that the really outstanding figures in history had the good fortune to be born at the right time. It is idle to guess at the way Beethoven might have developed had he been thrown into the musical scene a century earlier. The scene a century later could hardly have been the same without his influence. Fate, as he would have called it, could not have chosen a more propitious moment. Beethoven was born in 1770 at Bonn in the Rhineland: it was the right time – music was ready for him.

Nevertheless the value of art does not always move forward in an upward graph. We cannot say, as the nineteenth century tended to say, that Beethoven 'carried on where his predecessors left off', as though one might improve on Haydn or Mozart. Art does not respond to such reasoning, as the ever-increasing popularity of Mozart is there to remind us. Beethoven plumbed not greater but different depths: he represented a different type of artist, a different age. The age is sometimes called 'the advent of Romanticism', the trend towards freer and more personal expression. Yet we cannot call Beethoven a Romantic, for all our subjective involvement in his music. 'From the heart, may it go to the heart!' he wrote on the score of his *Missa Solemnis*. But he satisfies the intellect, the objective love of form, in equal measure: he never wavered in his allegiance to the classical ideals. His search for the ideal form cost him endless hard labour, as his sketch-books show: his first thoughts were often embarrassingly crude and commonplace, but he hammered them into shape with unflinching self-criticism. As a result, the force of his will is marked on almost every bar of his greatest works. He triumphed in a long, lonely battle not only against physical adversity but with the material of music itself. Much has been written about the moral strength of his music. Suffice it to say that his instinct and patience sifted away trivial and ephemeral emotions, capturing the noblest and most enduring. But the battle of the mind is still there to hear: we relive his tragedies and his triumphs as we listen to him.

Beethoven's influence was so great that even such opposites as

6

Brahms and Wagner paid homage to him. Wagner saw him as the precursor of music-drama, and launched the Bayreuth theatre to the sounds of the Ninth Symphony; Brahms, classically minded, could have pointed to Wagner's choice of the Ninth and not of Beethoven's one opera *Fidelio*. The Ninth, despite the explicit drama of the choral finale, owed most of its strength to the power of absolute music. It was in the classical forms that Beethoven's dramatic instinct thrived: in the symphony, the concerto, the string quartet, the sonata. These concepts he inherited. His influence may have been great—so great that we illogically speak of 'Beethovenish' passages in Mozart and Haydn – but his heritage was great too. To begin with, he inherited a musical language: one firmly rooted in tonality, and in which melodiousness and counterpoint could be generously interchanged and interwoven, the fusion of *galant* and learned styles that characterized the mature works of Haydn and Mozart. It brought with it established ideas of form and medium, ideas which Beethoven, for all his revolutionary manner, scarcely changed even though at times he stretched them almost to breaking-point. The orchestra had settled into a regular pattern of wind and strings, with the pair of timpani that inspired so many imaginative gestures; the quartet, basis of the orchestra's string section, had emerged as the most perfect chamber-music 'balance'; the piano itself had arrived, and its possibilities in concertos and chamber music had been fully explored. If 'fully' seems an extravagant word, we may ask whether Mozart's many piano concertos, or his two piano quartets, have ever been surpassed for their grasp of such new mediums.

The piano was, however, still in its infancy. But its assets had been seen and seized upon: Mozart's concertos, and the later sonatas of Haydn, were written with it, and not the harpsichord, in mind. The assets were obvious. When Cristofori introduced the instrument around 1710 he solved a problem that had beset keyboard-makers from the start: how to transmit expression from the fingers? The traditional harpsichords and clavichords had their pros and cons. The harpsichord scored in brilliance, boasting such luxuries as extra keyboards, alternative sets of quills, and octave-couplings: hence the grandeur of terraced dynamics, which made Bach's *Italian Concerto* possible on a solo instrument. But quills operated by remote control were unresponsive to finger-subtlety, which accounts for the profusion of ornaments and flourishes in early keyboard music – features that could be made rhythmically expressive. On the other hand the clavichord responded to the finger (its hammers or tangents both struck and stopped the string, encouraging the most delicate nuances and vibrato) – but its tone was useless in a large room. The piano-forte offered something of both these worlds: the escapement action, with its free-flying hammer, was the answer: the finger controlled the velocity, the velocity determined the tone. It had its teething troubles, but Bach, who never possessed one himself and began by being sceptical, praised the Silbermann models he met at the court of Frederick the Great in 1747 – enough to ease the conscience of the modern Bach pianist. Forty years later Mozart was renowned for his cantabile, which outshone many a prima donna's. The piano could sing, and it could produce instant dynamic gradations from the fingers. Without it the opening of Beethoven's first sonata could never have been written *this* way:

EX. 1

(Yet what an absurd abbreviation, pianoforte or fortepiano into piano! Common usage wins the day, however, even though we *do* call the *Appassionata* a 'soft' sonata.) But back to Bach: what did Beethoven in fact know of him? More than one might have expected in the dark days of neglect, when the *St Matthew Passion* still lay silent and forgotten, waiting for Mendelssohn to rediscover it. He knew and admired the 'old testament' of preludes and fugues, which had been placed in his hands by his early teacher, Christian Gottlob Neefe. His much later absorption in counterpoint might be traced back to this time, for he continued playing 'The 48' long after his arrival in Vienna, and something of his way with them can be traced in Czerny's dangerously personal edition. Meanwhile the fugue, which had been such a challenge for the composer and a fortress for the mind in Bach's day, had gone out of fashion: a great deal had happened in the half-century that separated the completion of Book Two of *The Well-tempered Clavier* (1744) from the publication of Beethoven's Op. 2 Sonatas (1796). For if the eighteenth-century had, in general, turned away from the learned style in favour of more easy-going entertainment music, serious composers still required a serious form to stir their minds as well as their hearts. The sonata and all its parallels – the symphony, the concerto, the quartet – provided the new fortress, and though the labels were old they soon acquired a special meaning.

Italy had lent its language to the world of music, and the term sonata had long been used to denote a piece to be played or 'sounded', as opposed to a 'cantata'. Giovanni Gabrieli in 1597 published *sonate* for a consort of wind and strings, and in the course of the next century the word was applied to works of very different kinds, though there was a growing tendency to limit it to extended compositions in contrasted 'movements'. (Even Domenico Scarlatti's one-movement harpsichord sonatas were, in many cases, intended to be played in pairs.) Bach, in the early eighteenth-century, was more specific when he differentiated between sonatas and suites (or partitas), the latter containing dance-forms, the former more serious allegros, adagios, and fugues. Yet, paradoxically enough, one dance-form, the minuet, found its way into the later 'classical' sonata, and the Beethoven scherzo derived from it. Thus terms and forms evolved from the demands of style, and the fittest survived. But the terms themselves could be misleading, such as the expression 'sonata form', which referred to a much-favoured design from the mid-eighteenth-century onwards. It flourished in the works of Bach's son, Philipp Emanuel, and after him in Haydn and Mozart, and it had far-reaching consequences. 'Sonata form' is a confusing term in that it describes the possible behaviour of a single movement, not a sonata as a whole, and from about 1740 the sonata *forms* leant heavily upon it, especially when a taut or arresting argument was involved, as in most classical first movements. But its use was not obligatory: Mozart made one of his best-known sonatas out of a set of variations, a minuet and a rondo (K.331). Neither, for that matter, did Beethoven hesitate to write sonatas in two, three or four movements; to begin, if needs

9

be, with a slow movement instead of an *allegro* (Op. 27 no. 2); or to end with one (Op. 109 or 111). Both composers were stricter in their approach to the symphony: the solo sonata was more intimate and more flexible. 'Sonata form', however, had such an influence on all instrumental music that its evolution is worth tracing.

The simplest tune tends to divide into halves by natural laws of gravitation and respiration. In this way 'binary form' came into being, and a greater purpose was served when the first half journeyed outwards to a new key (probably the dominant) and the second half returned home. Bach elaborated on this basic idea in his dance-movements, and Scarlatti in his one-movement sonatas, and the symmetry was underlined by the repeat of each half. Yet there developed a widespread tendency for the second 'half' to grow disproportionately and to show two distinct phases: an inclination to dally and explore on the homeward route, and, in view of this, the need to clinch the eventual arrival with a memory, in the home key, of the events of the outward journey. (Bach illustrated this perfectly in some of his second-book preludes in *The Well-tempered Clavier*, especially those in D major, F minor, and B flat major, even though history arranged that his sons, not he, should hand on the principle of exposition, development, and recapitulation to his successors.) Enlarge the time-scale, maybe, and throw in a more dramatic contrast of ideas to emphasize the existing contrast of keys – the familiar first and second subjects or 'groups' – and the genealogy is clear. Key was, however, the guiding factor: the *exposition*, starting from home, ended by establishing a new key and new ideas (the second subject); the *development* was unfettered, with continual modulation, but gravitated eventually to the *recapitulation*, which recalled the music of the exposition but within the gravitational field of the home key, and to this a coda might or might not be added. With innumerable modifications of one kind or another, this is the common denominator of hundreds of famous movements from the classical period onwards. It became the accepted first-movement form of sonatas and symphonies, but its implications were endless: slow movements and finales were just as likely to fall under its spell. By the time Beethoven arrived, sonata form was as much second nature to composers as the fugue had been to Bach.

Beethoven did not imbibe all these new influences at once. The

10

instruments of his childhood were still the harpsichord and its more modest cousin, the spinet (not to mention the organ); and the greatest works of Haydn and Mozart had yet to come. But Mozart's fame had reached Bonn to the extent that Beethoven's father had hopes, vain ones, of turning his son into a prodigy; and Beethoven, on his preliminary visit to Vienna, played to Mozart in 1787. 'Playing' in those days implied extemporizing on a given theme, and as this was Beethoven's speciality Mozart prophesied a great future for him. Plans to study with him came to nothing: by the time Beethoven returned (1792) Mozart, alas, was dead. Meanwhile Haydn had called at Bonn on his way to and from his London triumphs, and when Beethoven made his final departure, never to return to the Rhineland, his early friend and patron Count Waldstein (later immortalized in Op. 53) begged him to work hard in Vienna and to seek Mozart's spirit 'at the hands of Haydn'. The lessons with Haydn were not an unqualified success, and Beethoven undoubtedly learnt more from the composer than the teacher. Haydn was soon off to London again, and Beethoven sought the discipline of others: Johann Schenk, Albrechtsberger, Salieri, and Aloys Förster. He still remembered Neefe's influence, and wrote to him: 'Should I ever become a great man, you too will share in my success'. But Beethoven sought, above all, independence: his greatest teacher was to be his own experience. It taught him early on that enduring art must satisfy in opposite, complementary ways. There is the emotional impact of music – 'from the heart to the heart' – but there is also the desire to satisfy the mind and to arrange ideas in their most potent form. Call it, if you like, the architectural quality of music. Even the unskilled listener senses when a piece is well made, because the composer's struggle with form forces him to channel and to crystallize his thoughts. This awareness is apparent in the Op. 1 trios and the Op. 2 piano sonatas.

The opus numbers, incidentally, are a fair but not infallible guide to the order of Beethoven's works, since they refer to the order of publication and not completion: thus the 'Second' Piano Concerto, Op. 19, was an earlier work than the 'First', Op. 15. But the only misleading number in the piano sonatas is Op. 49, comprising two favourite 'easy' works which were held back for some years. Research into the sketches is helpful here, but the long and simultaneous gestation of different compositions makes it hard to assign exact dates. We know, however, that the three sonatas of Op. 2 were ready by 1795 and that they drew on some much earlier material too, in the slow movement of no. 1 and the first movement of no. 3. The group of three was dedicated to Haydn, but with no deferential verbiage. Perhaps Haydn was disappointed, but after three years in Vienna Beethoven had no need to defer. He was a master with a will of his own, and the piano had become his instinctive medium, winning him many entries into high society. He accepted patronage on his own terms: the situation had changed since the days of Bach, or the early days of Haydn, or even the more recent days of Mozart, who had suffered the tragedy of becoming a free-lance too soon. The tremors of the French Revolution were felt all over Europe and the new liberalism was reflected fearlessly in Beethoven's music. It was an age in which he could counter his brother's pretentious visiting-card, marked 'estate owner', with one marked 'brain owner'.

THE TURN OF THE CENTURY

THE SONATAS TO OP. 22

Sonata in F minor, Op. 2, no. 1

The opening of the first sonata has already been quoted in Ex. 1 as an example of Beethoven's personal use of abrupt dynamic changes. At a quick glance the theme looks Mozartean: the 'Mannheim rocket' that had set off the finale of the great G minor Symphony, though Mozart had in fact used a similar leaping figure in an earlier symphony in the same key, no. 25, before he heard the virtuosity of the Mannheim orchestra. (So, for that matter, did C. P. E. Bach – in a piano sonata in F minor.) This offers an interesting comparison. Mozart, for all his drama, clinched and rounded off his theme: Beethoven allows his its head, jumps forward to a fortissimo climax in no time at all, falls back exhausted, pauses, develops it more cautiously in another key altogether, and still reaches his second subject in record time. He did not always use such shock tactics from the start. The other sonatas of this group are both more precise and more spacious in their opening gestures, but this example shows how dangerous it is to underestimate 'early' Beethoven: no one could have guessed the dynamics from the bare notes. The movement lives up to its opening momentum, and is in the most compact sonata form, with no irrelevant note and no mere transposition for the recapitulation. Beethoven learnt from Mozart's minor-key works, in particular, of the special drama and pathos obtained from translating the second group of themes from relative major to tonic *minor* at this point. In his later works he often preferred to keep them in the major key, leaving the coda to bring back the minor; but here the coda is no more than a brusque interruption and extension of the final cadence. F minor and major rule this sonata. The *adagio*, in the major, derives from an early piano quartet and its texture suggests the richness of conversing strings at times: its serene beauty is disturbed by some stabbing minor-ninth dissonances, a Mozartean trait, but the pianistic variants of the opening phrase owe more to Haydn. Minor and major alternate in the minuet and trio, and there is no happy ending to the finale. It is a stormscape, forerunner of Op. 27, no. 2, and Op. 57, and the lead back from the long central 'consoling' cantilena is, already, a masterly example of the art of mood-transition.

13

Sonata in A, Op. 2, no. 2

Beethoven's ability to pack immense energy and meaning into a mere handful of notes is illustrated by the index of opening bars given in most editions of the sonatas. Or is this being wise after the event? The smallest rhythmic germ might dominate a whole movement, and Beethoven's fame as an extempore player no doubt owed a great deal to his gift of developing much out of little. But in composition the basic figures were often distilled from long forethought: the first phrases of the F major Quartet, Op. 18, no. 1, seemingly spontaneous, were reshaped again and again. So was Op. 2, no. 1; but, so far as I know, nothing survives of the sketches for nos. 2 and 3. Who could have foreseen, however, that the playful opening of no. 2 would lead, halfway through the exposition, to such dramatic exchanges as these?

EX. 2

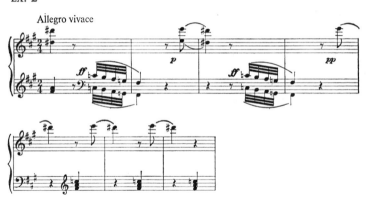

But, despite this resource, the A major is on a much grander time-scale than the F minor: it might even be thought garrulous by comparison, but its topics are plentiful, and the first movement development, leaving few stones unturned, is in proportion. There are daring strettos and skips to tax the player, and daring enharmonic twists in the second subject; but the slow movement, unusually marked *largo appassionato*, contains the heart of the work. Its nobly simple theme calls for an orchestral sonority of horns with a pizzicato bass: a touchstone for the performer's imagination.

All the Op. 2 sonatas have four movements, as though in

14

preparation for the accepted scale of the symphony. Mozart and Haydn between them had decided that three, or even two, sufficed for a sonata. The larger forces demanded more room to spread themselves, for as a general rule the duet and the trio sided with the sonata, the quartet with the symphony. The concerto, content with three movements, enlarged the canvas automatically with its rivalry of solo and orchestra, and the minuet, or scherzo, was less suited to antiphonal treatment (though Brahms was to offer one long-delayed solution in his four-movement B flat Concerto many years later). To return to the A major Sonata: the minuet has become prophetically a scherzo – not the volatile scherzo one associates with Beethoven but an *allegretto* that begins innocently and ends defiantly. Dynamics have played their part again, and even the pleading minor-key trio section rises in a few bars from piano to fortissimo. The final rondo is not brilliant but *grazioso*, and the widely circling leaps and florid decorations forbid any sense of haste. There is a more aggressive middle episode, with which the rondo-theme links up unexpectedly at the end, but the close itself is poetic and peaceful.

Sonata in C, Op. 2, no. 3

The C major, third of the group, is beloved of virtuoso pianists for its outward glitter. It has often suffered at their hands: there is a temptation to rattle off its passage-work and to reduce the finale to a breath-taking study in staccato sixths. How rarely do we hear even the first bars of this sonata worthily realized, in time and texture? The four-part writing suggests, as so often with Beethoven, a string quartet, with the 'cello taking the lead in the eighth bar; until the first fortissimo breaks in unheralded, like a great orchestral tutti. All this is lost if the player is careless or unobservant or makes an unauthorized crescendo. Nevertheless brilliance is the key-note, even to the extent of a six-four chord and a brief written-in cadenza in the coda. The fortissimo passage-work is built with common bricks, arpeggios and broken octaves – 'the rattling of the dishes at a royal feast' in Wagner's words – but it is delivered with a youthful exultance, and there is plenty to satisfy the mind in Beethoven's endless play with the first subject. Once again the *adagio* is superb in its exploitation of new keyboard colours, and as it is in the exotic key of E major those sensitive to long-term key relations will note the splendidly dramatic effect when the main theme is thundered out in C major,

15

the key of all the other movements. The scherzo, a real *allegro* this time, starts with modestly fugal ambitions but abandons them for the pleasure of developing a syncopated chordal figure: this is cut short by an abrupt gesture that gives rise, after the trio and the return of the scherzo, to a coda that expires, pianissimo, in the bass. The finale, beginning with the virtuoso flight of sixths, has the most Beethovenish coda of all, full of pauses, key-surprises, and false starts, ending with a sudden 'down to earth'. Haydn enjoyed such shocks, too.

In form the finale, like that of the preceding sonata, is that fascinating cross-breed the 'sonata-rondo', much favoured in Mozart's concerto-finales. Beethoven followed suit in all of his concertos and in many, but by no means all, of his sonatas. The 'simple' rondo had implied no more than the coming round of a main theme, with intervening episodes that were under no obligation to show any relationship to it or to one another: the textbooks show it as A–B–A–C–A etc. Such a happy-go-lucky affair could hardly satisfy the serious composer writing a serious work, and yet the rondo principle was attractive. It offered an alternative, more relaxed, form; and it suited the mood of many finales, where an outstanding recurring theme could in fact win the day and the applause. But how to organize the episodes and give them purpose? It was here that sonata form stepped in: 'Allow for three episodes. But treat the first and the last as a second subject with the usual contrast of key, leaving the middle one free either for development or for quite new material, according to choice.' In this way the threads of the rondo, or sonata-rondo, were tightened: A–B–A–C–A–B–A, with the essential difference of key between B^1 and B^2. This was learnt, or adopted, from sonata form. Forms are not cut-and-dried affairs, but can influence and enrich one another.

Sonata in E flat, Op. 7

Op. 7 also ends with a spacious sonata-rondo. It followed close on the heels of the Op. 2 set: a solitary work, dating from 1796 and inscribed to a pupil, the Countess Babette von Keglevics. Beethoven's susceptibility to women, regardless of station, was matched by theirs to him and led to the work being nicknamed at one time 'Die Verliebte'. The original published title 'Grande Sonate' has more meaning. The sonata is indeed on a grand scale, and the first movement marking, *molto allegro e con brio*, hints

16

at an unusual outburst of vigour and passion. It sweeps forward irresistibly on a tide of six-eight quavers, carrying with it a whole chain of ideas, some rhythmic, some lyrical. The frequent use of sequences, and of elementary harmony to establish a key, serves to pin-point the drama of the sudden departure. A simple gesture can be dramatic when it unlocks a new door or points in a new direction, as happens at the close of the first paragraph and again at the start of the development: these abrupt plunges into new keys show that form is 'harmony writ large' as Tovey would have put it. Yet the opening looks simple enough on paper: a proud but passionate affirmation of the chord of E flat.

In the second movement measured silence becomes as eloquent as sound (one thinks forward to the *Introduzione* of the *Waldstein*), and there is a magic turning from C major to A flat for a second, more aspiring theme. (One thinks of the first movement of Op. 110.) The last four bars make the silences audible, with rich new harmony; the slow movements, above all, show early Beethoven at its maturest. The third movement is a cross between minuet and scherzo, the main part drawing gentle elegant contours out of the common chord, the trio full of menacing triplets and mysterious eruptions. In the finale, as in Op. 2, no. 2, there is little conventional brilliance: the sonata-rondo theme is tender and flowing, and seems, with its love of dominant harmony, to have been caught in mid-flight. But its second strain leads to a pause on octave B flats, innocent enough at the start but carrying infinite possibilities for Beethoven's impulsive dramatic sense. After the first return of the rondo it slips upward through B natural into C minor for a fiery middle episode, but in the coda a similar move brings instead a far-away echo of the rondo-theme itself in a far-away key. At the end the links are strengthened when the stormy C minor music sails in calmly in the home key: the lion returns like a lamb. This affectionate warm-hearted sonata is seldom played. Why? Because it ends so unsensationally on an intimate tender note?

Sonata in C minor, Op. 10, no. 1

Op. 10 consists of three sonatas again. They were sketched and developed between 1796 and 1798, and the first two have been understandably overshadowed by the magnificence of the third, in D major. But the first of the group is in the significant key of C minor, a special one not only for Beethoven but, as he himself

17

noted, for Mozart. 'We shall never be able to live up to this', he said, or words to that effect, when listening to the finale of Mozart's C minor Concerto, and presumably he also admired his C minor Sonata, which was published as early as 1785. Mozart began with a dramatic, operatic alternation of masculine and feminine elements, forte and piano; and he leapt, like Beethoven, into C *major* at the development, but shattered the effect of triumph by turning the music, immediately and ironically, towards F minor. The parallel with Op. 10, no. 1 is remarkable, but a little unfair. Beethoven could not yet match Mozart on his own ground, and the form is more rough-hewn. There are compensations in the youthful impetuosity and the impulsiveness that led him to recapitulate the second subject in the 'wrong' key and then to 'correct' himself – another foretaste of the *Waldstein*. The first theme has the strength of a spring rapidly uncoiling upwards, and is good practice for pianists, but unlike the bold steps of Mozart's its energy exhausts it. There is no coda: simply two peremptory chords. The *adagio* has lofty intentions but a certain stiffness of phrase and manner that is resolved only in the calm, melting coda; and the finale relates a breathless series of events in full sonata form but at a hectic *prestissimo* tempo. The shadow of fate – alias the Fifth Symphony, also in C minor – is never far away, and the sudden reappearance of the second subject theme in D flat, of all keys, belies the fact that the end is near at hand.

Sonata in F, Op. 10, no. 2

Both the C minor and the F major sonatas revert to the three-movement plan. This apart, they could hardly be more different, for key-associations played a strong part, however sub-consciously, in Beethoven's music. C minor was intensely dramatic, as we have just seen and shall soon see again in Op. 13; F major was a relaxed, open-air key, the key of the *Pastoral* Symphony to come. This is a rash generalization, but the common traits are too many for pure chance. Edwin Fischer remarked that the mock-fugal finale of Op. 10, no. 2, reminded him both of Bach's F major Two-part Invention and of the second move-ment of Beethoven's First Symphony. To which we might add that the F major Bagatelle from Op. 33 shows a certain family likeness, too: its play with F major *vis-à-vis* D major links up with the *Pastoral* scherzo, and the false reprise in *D major*

18

of the sonata's first movement completes an enchanted circle.

Whereas the C minor owed much to Mozart, formally at any rate, the F major suggests Haydn, even from the look of the notes on the page. This time the slow movement is sacrificed, but the *allegretto* that replaces it has its own emotional depths: Schubert, surely, must have admired the trio with its stabbing left-hand accents protesting against the blandness of the D flat theme? As for the finale, mentioned above, it resembles a bucolic revelry of wind instruments, with a bassoon setting off the fugato and collecting all the players together over a drone-bass for a second, cadence theme. Yet despite its miniature sonata form there is in reality no second theme as such; one sprightly motive dominates all, which is also a Haydnish rather than a Mozartean practice.

Sonata in D, Op. 10, no. 3

The splendours of the D major Sonata place it in a higher category altogether. Some of the keyboard patterns can be traced to the influence of Clementi, whose new pianistic style was known in Bonn before Beethoven left there, but the architectural certainty and economy are Beethoven's own from start to finish. Who else could have extracted such meaning from the first four notes of the unison opening subject?

EX. 3

Clever analysts have even found the finale theme hidden in the *next* three notes. But intentional allusions between, as opposed to within, movements were rare in Beethoven, and it would be hard to find a piece that avoided touching such a motive in passing. The downward half-scale is quite another matter, as a glance at the score shows it turning up continually in various guises, blossoming into long paragraphs, combining, unifying, and, when form demands it, beckoning back the whole subject. The slow movement (it almost goes without saying by this time) makes the

19

sonata a great one. Even those sceptical of the power of absolute music to convey specific emotions must sense the grief-laden atmosphere, the quiet heaviness of the chords that pull the theme earthwards, the anguished outbursts, the final extinction of hope. Or we may look at it another way, as a study in deep sonorities and changes of register, as a sonata-form movement in slow six-eight time with a new theme instead of a development (F major) and a massive coda in which the home key wins on all dynamic levels (D minor). Beethoven marked it *largo e mesto*, and 'mesto' means sad or gloomy. Was it written from a general observation of life, or as an expression of personal grief, an unhappy love-affair, the memory of his mother's death, or a premonition of his own deafness? The craft of composition alone cannot account for the overtones, any more than it can explain the pathos of Mozart's minor-key *andantes* and *adagios*. This *largo* strikes deeper than anything Beethoven had composed up to that time.

The D major Sonata has four movements. Perhaps Beethoven had already conceived ideas for the capricious rondo before the *largo* had developed such overwhelming significance. Something else was needed to bridge the gap: a minuet of classical cast, lyrical in feeling and owing a debt to the 'compassionate' second subject in Mozart's D minor Concerto, a work Beethoven loved to the extent of writing cadenzas for it. The trio is witty and full of quick repartee, but by now we have adjusted to the world of daylight and are ready to enjoy the Haydnish humour of the rondo-finale, with its ubiquitous, questioning three-note motive.

Grande sonate pathétique, in C minor, Op. 13

In the *Pathétique* we meet the first of the sonatas to have acquired a universal popularity. The full title was Beethoven's own: it was thus spared the embarrassment of the nickname the famous *adagio* must surely have earned for it. It was composed in 1798 and published in the following year, and the key is again the 'dramatic' C minor. Popularity has been known to breed contempt unfairly, for Op. 13 is infinitely more arresting than its predecessor in Op. 10; more passionate and challenging, more controlled and integrated, and more assured in its moods. It no longer takes Mozart as a model, but owes something to the emotional style of Dussek, whose sonatas are perhaps more interesting for their prophecies than their intrinsic value.

20

The powerfully dramatic prelude to the first movement is far more than an introduction, playing such a part in the development and the coda that there are grounds for including it in the customary repeat of the exposition. This makes the pause before the repeat meaningful, especially since the second-time pause leads to a return of the *grave* in G minor. Surely these should balance? Moreover Beethoven did not enclose the *allegro* with a reverse repeat-sign, though most editors have 'corrected' the 'omission'. The essence and originality of the movement lie in this alternation of *grave* and *allegro di molto e con brio*: one is tempted to quote the much later Beethoven of the Op. 135 Quartet, 'Muss es sein? Es muss sein!' (Must it be? It must be!), to underline the unity of the contrast. The driving force of the *allegro* itself allows no respite in the second group of themes, beginning with an agitated duologue between bass and treble: the wide key-scheme embraces here E flat minor and, later, through a magic enharmonic change in the *grave* music, E minor, the development then absorbing and transmuting the *grave* theme in *allegro* tempo. Edwin Fischer, who played the sonata magnificently, criticized the orchestral nature of the piano writing. This was just: the first movement seems symphonically conceived, from the *fp* chords at the start to the smouldering left-hand 'timpani rolls' that accompany much of the *allegro*. It was not of this movement that Beethoven said 'the piano must break!' but it might well have been, considering the instruments of his time.

The *adagio cantabile* was once a prey to arrangers and derangers. Beethoven made no attempt to develop the theme: he recognized its direct emotional appeal and accepted the simplest of rondo forms. Was it accidental that when Mozart anticipated the first two bars in the *adagio* of his C minor, and when Brahms remembered the next two in his Op. 5, both composers turned to A flat and the same deep-singing register of the piano? In Beethoven's *adagio* there are two episodes: a brief interlude in which an eloquent solo voice rises aloft, and a more agitated section whose triplet rhythm eventually adapts itself to the original theme. The third and final movement is a sonata-rondo with an elusive character, part wistful, part defiant. The episodes are more conciliatory, but they all end by being drawn back into the C minor atmosphere. In the coda, a further excursion is suggested, only to be cast aside by an abrupt reaffirmation of the key.

Beethoven, we are told, played the rondo-theme 'humorously'.

21

What do we know of his playing? Cherubini described it as 'rough', Cramer found it 'inconsistent and muddled', but all agree that it was full of character and temperament, with a vehemence that increased with his growing deafness until, as Marion Scott summed it up, 'a fantasia from him was enough to put a piano out of action'. Schindler, his factotum in later years, went into details. We learn from him that Beethoven had no use for 'miniature painting', but demanded firm accentuation, a sustained tone in cantabile, and strength of expression at all times. The singing style he inherited from Mozart through Clementi. He criticized the virtuoso manner of the young Czerny, despite the latter's advocacy of his works. Schindler's more detailed memories of Beethoven's playing read rather amusingly today: 'His manner of holding down particular notes, combined with a kind of soft gliding touch, imparted such a vivid colouring that the hearer could fancy he actually beheld the lover in his living form, and heard him apostrophizing his obdurate mistress'. The work in question was the gentle intimate G major Sonata, Op. 14, no. 2.

Sonata in E, Op. 14, no. 1
Sonata in G, Op. 14, no. 2

The Op. 14 sonatas are a pair, and Richter played them as such at a London recital in 1963. His intimate manner suited them, for they resist any attempt at the grand manner. Beethoven often relaxed in this way from a stormy mood to a gentle one, but although the sonatas appeared soon after the *Pathétique* they may have been sketched as early as 1795. The first, in E major, interested him enough for him to make a string quartet arrangement in F major, and the quartet texture, common enough in Beethoven's piano music, stares up from the opening lines, though the last-movement theme caused some drastic rethinking. Richter took the second movement at a leisurely *andante*: Beethoven is supposed to have attacked it *allegro furioso*, which all goes to show how ambiguous the term *allegretto* can be. The G major Sonata is even more confiding and affectionate, with a miniature set of variations on a march-like tune for the middle movement. Both sonatas have three movements, but the finales could not be more different within their scale. The E major has a sonata-rondo, mellifluous, with one brief display of strength at the end; the G major an out-and-out scherzo in straight rondo-form, with a theme that scampers across the bar-lines, delighted in the discovery that thrice two equals twice three. There is no possible place for a profound *adagio* in these endearing works, and for a return to the grander scale we must look to the next sonata, Op. 22.

Sonata in B flat, Op. 22

By 1800, significant year, Beethoven had achieved a good deal in consolidating his style and his reputation. In chamber music: the Op. 1 Piano Trios, the Op. 5 'Cello Sonatas, the Op. 9 String Trios, the Op. 12 Violin Sonatas, culminating in the Op. 18 String Quartets; in the orchestral sphere, the first three piano concertos and, an important landmark, the First Symphony; in solo piano works, the first eleven sonatas. These were the main arteries, but there were other works too – the Quintet for wind and piano, the Horn Sonata, the Septet. In all these the classical forms held good. Beethoven wrote to Nikolaus Zmeskall, his friend in the Hungarian Chancellery: 'Do please send me one or two quills, for I am really extremely short of them. . . .'

Yet the one sonata of the year, Op. 22, has dropped out of the repertoire. Beethoven was confident of its success, but the work's own confidence leads to a certain predictability. It is in fact surprisingly free from surprises, and stands firmly at the crossroads without committing itself to any new departure. The four-movement plan is worked out with astonishing regularity of form and key, with few of the daring relationships and sudden impulses we find, for instance, in Op. 7 or Op. 10, no. 3. In the first movement sonata form is carried through with such precision that Beethoven, who loved codas, adds no extra note for once, a '*tour de force* in punctuality' – to quote Tovey's delightful simile – 'as when an oarsman's last stroke brings his boat to the landing-stage and enables him to ship sculls, throw the painter to the waterman, and step on shore in the same moment'. There are, however, fascinating mutations of the slow movement theme in the development, but such harmonic complexes were well known to Mozart. This is not to belittle the work's originality, for the ideas of the first movement have a typical Beethovenish clarity, the minuet has its abrupt dynamic contrasts, and the mild sonata-rondo (a cousin of the F major Violin Sonata's) a tense, stern development for the middle episode. It is, all in all, a work of deliberate consolidation, gathering strength from convention. The strength was soon required – and provided.

THE MIDDLE PERIOD
OP. 26 TO THE 'APPASSIONATA'

One can seldom say of any creative artist's work, 'Here the early period stops, here the middle begins'. The dividing-line, convenient for reference, is bound to be arbitrary when the growth is consistent, and crooked when the works are plentiful. Nevertheless 1800 is a useful date for Beethoven: he completed his conquest of instrumental forms with the symphony. Had he looked into the future he could hardly have foreseen that he would compose the *Eroica*, an epoch-making work if ever there was one, within another four years. The epoch-making quality was as much expressive and spiritual as technical and architectural, and we cannot but relate it to personal events. His hearing had already deteriorated, and his letters to Amenda and Wegeler in the summer of 1801 show him in the depths of despair, the unhappiest of God's creatures. It was a year before the crisis of the Heiligenstadt Testament. At Heiligenstadt Beethoven contemplated death, but his inner ear and his love of art gave him life, twenty-five more years of the richest creation.

Sonata in A flat, Op. 26
There was no sudden *Eroica* among the piano sonatas, and the independent variations that sometimes bear its name derive from a common source, the *Prometheus* ballet-music: the *Eroica* finale was to use the same theme and some of the same procedures. This is incidental, but variation-form appears in the next sonata on the list, Op. 26 in A flat, completed in 1801. Here, quite unlike Op. 22, the order of events is unusual in the extreme: variations for the first movement, scherzo second, a funeral march 'for the death of a hero' (this does sound prophetic), and a rippling finale in sonata-rondo form. The variation technique had often played a subsidiary role in sonata movements – a rondo theme might be 'varied' on its return, a slow movement theme might invite embellishments – but only one Beethoven piano sonata, Op. 14, no. 2, had so far included a *set* of variations and only three more were to do so: the *Appassionata*, Op. 109 and Op. 111, the last two raising the art to its sublimest level. Mozart, however, had begun his A major Sonata with an *andante* and variations, and Beethoven's Op. 26 does the same. The theme – to which a Schubert

24

Impromptu in the same key has a certain likeness – is a ternary one: that is to say it has its own middle section and turns back on itself, a feature that Beethoven, who always approached this form with classical strictness, observed faithfully in the variations. They are five in number, each one bringing a new mood and a new pattern of notes, but the theme itself never seems far away, and the short, free coda seems like an extension of it.

The scherzo could hardly come after the funeral march, so it is placed second. (The *Eroica* scherzo does follow the march, but it begins with a mere whispering whereas this one has biting sforzati from the start.) The march itself, in A flat minor, is purposely monotonous in the sombre dotted rhythm favoured by such pieces – compare Chopin's – but it is marked by extraordinary enharmonic modulations, 'enharmonic' being the technical term for the alchemy through which Beethoven approaches a note as G flat and leaves it as F sharp, thereby opening up new harmonic avenues. The finale, a toccata in all but name, ripples unconcernedly: it is an excellent study for the pianist, and turns a technical device of broken chords to musical ends.

Sonata in E flat, Op. 27, no. 1
Sonata in C sharp minor, Op. 27, no. 2 (Moonlight)

The next two sonatas of 1801 carry the unorthodox arrangement of movements still further, but both disarm criticism with the subtitle 'quasi una fantasia'. The first, in E flat, has none the less been criticized for its 'commonplace' opening movement. On paper the music looks childlike: a squarely-phrased, sectional *andante* with an incongruous *allegro* trio in the unsympathetically related key of C major. Edwin Fischer told how he too was perplexed by this movement until he heard it played by a young girl 'with a naturalness, gentleness, equanimity and sadness that suggested that this was a true expression of some hidden suffering'. Seen in this way the music has the deceptive simplicity of Mozart's later works; played with forced expression, it is meaningless. The movements in this strangely personal sonata are to be played without a break: after the opening *andante*-cum-*allegro* an ominous shadowy scherzo in C minor; next, an *adagio*, reminiscent of the Third Piano Concerto, that closes into the finale but reappears on the last page, before the *presto* coda.

No such complexities and interrelations beset the second

25

'fantasy sonata' in C sharp minor. It also begins, unusually, with a slow movement: but its unity is obvious and fame has made it impervious to criticism. Beethoven did not call it the *Moonlight*, but the title is appropriate enough for the first movement and there is no need to be snobbish about it. By a natural law of compensation, works which are over-popular with one generation tend to be slighted by the next, but it is high time we freed ourselves from prejudice and discovered the *Moonlight* afresh. Abolish the title if it offends; but do not let this mislead us into thinking that Beethoven denied such pictorial associations. He often disclosed the source of his inspirations to his friends. Was the Juliet of the tomb-scene that reputedly inspired the slow movement of the first Op. 18 Quartet the Giulietta Guicciardi to whom the *Moonlight* is dedicated, and did the *agitato* finale express Beethoven's rage at being jilted? The music transcends the importance of such localized conjectures.

The *adagio sostenuto*, probably the most celebrated single movement Beethoven ever wrote, makes its entire effect through restraint and shows how well he understood the singing qualities of the piano at its quietest levels. For the performer 'senza sordini' meant 'without dampers' and referred to the use of the right, not the left, pedal (or the knee-lever found on early pianos). People will continue to argue over the degree of compromise required on a modern concert-grand: some pianists ignore Beethoven's long-held pedal effects; a few, like Schnabel, have taken them literally, as indicating a veiled, cloudy texture. Surely Schnabel erred, if he did in fact err, on the right side, for why should Beethoven mark them if they were ineffective on his instruments? He seldom indicated normal pedalling, and special instructions warrant special effects, as when the recitatives in the D minor Sonata, Op. 31, no. 2, rise 'like a voice from a tomb'. It is up to the individual to decide when half-pedalling is desirable, but any changes dictated by the slow-moving harmonies of the *Moonlight* should be imperceptible: daylight, in fact, should not be let in. Formally, though it seems like one continuous melody, the *adagio* can be analysed into the usual first-movement phases, with a short coda. But the quiet triplet accompaniment pervades all: in the development it holds the stage alone and climbs aloft in sequences; at the end it vanishes into the darkest regions of the bass. The *allegretto* breaks the spell gently, an offspring of the minuet and by no means as trivial as some players make it: there is a sense of

26

unrest in its syncopations, despite the relief of the major key. In the finale the urgency of the music demands the full drama of sonata form: it is another stormscape, and even the more humanly passionate second subject brings no respite. It dominates the development section and builds up a tremendous climax in the coda. There is a climactic pause, a cadenza, and a brief lull; but the last bars, in a favourite phrase of Sir Henry Wood's, 'rush onward to their doom'.

Sonata in D, Op. 28 (Pastorale)

The year 1801 produced one more sonata. Unlike the Sixth Symphony it was not given its popular name by Beethoven, but its predominantly sunlit character, as opposed to moonlit, inspired the publisher Cranz to christen it *Pastorale*. According to Czerny it was a favourite of Beethoven's and he needed no encouragement to play it, especially the second movement, the least 'pastoral' of the four. But both the first and last movements hover over the same repeated bass-note in their opening themes, and this was considered a rustic device. A remarkable feature of the first movement is the way in which the entire development section appears to grow out of one phrase of the first subject:

EX. 4

But by now we have learnt to expect such economy from Beethoven, and it enabled him to be prodigal elsewhere – in the generously flowing paragraphs of the second subject, for instance. These close into a cadence theme that looks on paper like a waltz with misplaced bar-lines: in performance it can sound dangerously like a waltz, and to counter this illusion there is some evidence that Beethoven intended a faint repercussion of the tied notes. This effect has been called a *Bebung* (literally, a trembling), but the piano, unlike the clavichord, cannot make a note vibrate through finger-pressure after it has been struck: all the pianist can do is to catch it on the rebound, as though the tie were a short slur, a secret used magically in the recitative of Op. 110.

The second movement begins with a simple, rather melancholy

27

song over a quasi-pizzicato bass, an effective combination of right-hand legato and a left-hand staccato that Beethoven had used in the slow movements of Op. 2, no. 2 and Op. 7. The key is D minor, and he felt no need to avoid the tonic major when the song gave way to a dance: on its return the song embellishes its repeats with passage-work, and a coda recalls the dance-figure, which sounds menacing in the minor key. Dynamics are the essence of the miniature, playful scherzo, while its trio clings obstinately to the same little phrase, humorously reversing its cadences in the second half. The finale is a sonata-rondo, so that we can renew acquaintance with its second group as well as its opening pastoral dance, which returns with subtle and delightful variants. Its lilting bass also has its say in the development and coda, and leaps, rather than lilts, in the brilliant *più allegro* ending. More serious matters, and contrapuntal discussion of them, arise during the episodic part of the development but cast only a temporary shadow over this happy sonata. Happy or not, it was not long afterwards that Beethoven wrote in a sketch-book: 'God knows why my piano music still makes the worst impression on me, especially when it is badly played!' Perhaps the clue is in the second part of the sentence. Or perhaps we should take seriously his remark to Krumpholz, about this time, that he intended to make a fresh start?

Sonata in G, Op. 31, no. 1

There are three sonatas in Op. 31, and of these no. 2, the D minor, is the masterpiece. Beside it the G major is uneventful, showing little sign of the 'new' Beethoven – or is it, in fact? The first movement, which seems at times to be making bricks without straw, has some interesting structural devices – a sudden leap from G to F major in the first theme, and an unexpected turn to B major instead of D for the second group, which comes back in E major in the recapitulation and then corrects itself by slipping through E minor to the home key. This rather dry analysis reveals an extraordinary parallel to the behaviour of the later *Waldstein* (a lesser work has often been known to pioneer for a greater one), and though the material itself is spare there are some picturesque minor-major changes that an unsuspecting listener might attribute to Schubert, who was however only six years old when this sonata was published:

EX. 5

There is something of Schubert's heavenly length, too, in the other two movements: in the *adagio grazioso*, which elaborates on a common enough melodic formula in a richly pianistic manner that looks forward to the Romantics; and in the rondo-finale, which spreads itself at leisure until the dying echoes of the theme are suddenly whisked away in a *presto* coda, just as they are in Schubert's great A major Sonata.

Sonata in D minor, Op. 31, no. 2

'Heavenly length' is certainly no term to apply to the tense drama of the D minor Sonata. When Schindler asked Beethoven what it 'meant', the master told him to read Shakespeare's *The Tempest*. Though this is sometimes written off as a stupid reply to a stupid question there may yet be something in it: Prospero, for instance, could be read into the mysterious bars of *largo* that cast recurring spells over the opening movement. Their subsequent translation into one of the *allegro* themes is perhaps the best nutshell example of Beethoven drawing immense significance out of a common chord through sheer will-power:

EX. 6

The tautness of the argument is apparent from the very first line of the work and makes an interesting comparison with that earlier

29

dual-tempo movement in the *Pathétique*. Here in the D minor the brief quotation above is enough to establish an air of mystery, and less than four bars of *allegro* suffice to set the whole conflict of moods and ideas before us, after which another key is propounded. Both these 'mysteries', for want of a better word, give rise to the famous 'voice from the tomb-vault' recitatives in the recapitulation, passages which depend on an imaginative realization of Beethoven's pedal marks and lose everything if drily played. Once under way, the *allegro* parts of the movement have the drive and the compactness of the first movement of the Fifth Symphony. There are, however, no consoling themes: the second subject, in the dominant minor, continues in the turbulent mood of the first, leaving emotional contrast for the return of the *largo*. It was at the height of the storm that Beethoven is supposed to have said 'the piano must break!'

One passage shows Beethoven turning to magnificent account the very limitations of the piano of his day. All the sonatas up to and including Op. 31 were written for a keyboard that stopped at the third F above middle C, and Beethoven welcomed the subsequent extensions with enthusiasm. But these stirring dissonances in the first movement of Op. 31, no. 2, would hardly have occurred to him if he had been able to carry the top voice upwards in octaves:

EX. 7

There are consolation and repose in the second movement, an *adagio* notoriously hard to bring off in performance on account of the wide 'vocal' leaps of the first theme and the insidious left-hand figure that drums its way through the transition. Like some other classical *adagios* it adapts sonata form to its expanded time-scale by omitting a development, in any case inappropriate for such song-like ideas, and by taking a short cut back to the opening material. The final *allegretto* is in the fullest sonata form with a

30

long development and a coda almost as extensive. It is unique in its relentless pursuit of a haunted tragic mood, with scarcely a gleam of a major key. Although it has suggested the galloping of a horse to some hearers, its predominant character is pathetic rather than energetic, the pursued rather than the pursuer, offset by occasional frenzied outbursts. The D minor Sonata, a landmark in the series, is the most personal musical document of the 'Heiligenstadt year'.

Sonata in E flat, Op. 31, no. 3

The third of the group is in absolute contrast, a reaction and relaxation not only of mood but of form in the larger sense of the word, for although it reverts to four movements it has no place for an *andante* or an *adagio* but incorporates both a scherzo (albeit in two-four time and with a leisurely gait despite its rapid-sounding footsteps) and a minuet – of the most moderate melodious type, with an equally moderate trio of swinging chords (which led Saint-Saëns to swing them into a set of variations for two pianos). The most striking moment in the sonata is its opening, where an ambiguous added-sixth chord on the subdominant resolves itself through a series of halting steps, rhythmically and harmonically, towards the tonic:

EX. 8

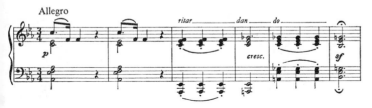

This process is not merely introductory: it is the first subject proper and is developed as such, harmonic progression and all. But as the very first chord carries its own fragment of melody, a falling fifth in a dotted rhythm that soon sets off a more positive theme *on* the tonic, this might be called the 'motto' of the movement. Elsewhere the manner is conventional, even *galant* – a divertimento by comparison with the previous sonata, no doubt – and this is borne out by the rest of the work, the scherzo, the minuet, and the vigorous six-eight 'hunting' finale.

31

Sonata in G minor, Op. 49, no. 1
Sonata in G, Op. 49, no. 2

The two little sonatas of Op. 49 were written much earlier, as has been mentioned – probably in 1796. A pair of movements suffices for each, and the Septet of 1800 borrowed the minuet of the second one. Despite their slightness they carry the authentic fingerprints – as do Beethoven's *Bagatelles*, his own favourite word for unpretentious miniatures. Even if they were not slight, however, they would be completely overshadowed by the two great sonatas which were shortly to follow, in order of opus numbers.

The *Waldstein* and the *Appassionata* form the two middle peaks of the whole range of the piano sonatas and demand detailed discussion. Between them lurks a strange and strangely-neglected work, the F major, Op. 54. All three sonatas date from 1804 and if Beethoven had written no more for the piano we might still have felt that his life-work in this genre was complete. As it turned out, he wrote no more piano sonatas for five years, but as he had completed no fewer than twenty-three in the previous nine years pianists can hardly complain.

Sonata in C, Op. 53 (Waldstein)

This sonata was dedicated to Beethoven's faithful patron, Count Waldstein: hence its nickname. Among the factors that contributed to its unprecedented grandeur of manner was the composer's acquisition in 1803 of an Erard piano, with an extended upward compass. This also led to his rewriting of certain passages in the C minor Concerto, though he did not to our knowledge retouch the earlier sonatas. Secondly, his style had become expansive in other directions: the *Kreutzer* Violin Sonata was composed in 1803, the *Eroica* Symphony early in 1804, and *Leonora* (alias *Fidelio*) was soon to follow. The *Eroica* enlarged the time-scale of sonata form in particular, and its first movement matched the scale with long-term planning of dynamics and key-relationships. Not that the *Waldstein* is long by the clock: hardly as long as Op. 7 in E flat. But for a three-movement sonata it promised to be, until Beethoven foresaw the danger of preceding an unusually spacious rondo with a fully-worked *andante* on more conventional lines. This he rejected – it survives as the independent *Andante favori* – and in its place he wrote a shorter, but more profound, *adagio Introduzione* to the finale. The struggle for greater

32

unity within a work as a whole showed itself in many such links between slow movements and finales in middle-period Beethoven – in the last two piano concertos, in the Violin Concerto, in the first *Razumovsky* quartet, and in the *Appassionata*. The Fifth and Sixth Symphonies also made their finales the outcome of the previous movements. But the device did not become a habit and it was always worked differently: the *Waldstein* rondo steals in, pianissimo; the *Appassionata* finale breaks in dramatically, fortissimo. Neither did Beethoven much favour any obvious borrowings between different movements – the examples can be counted on one hand. There may be subtle and even subconscious relationships, but in Beethoven the sanctity and integrity of movements was the general rule.

Let virtuosos please note that all three movements of the *Waldstein* begin pianissimo and that one of its commonest marks is *sempre pp*. Slack traditions have probably played more havoc with this sonata than any other, especially in matters of tempo and dynamics. Dynamics in Beethoven indicated far more than light and shade: they revealed the contours, the hills and valleys, of the landscape. As for consistency of tempo, Tovey must be quoted again: 'All the pianistic traditions that make thunder and lightning of the opening, and that read the E major theme as an *andante religioso*, are mere disguises of fatigue.' The need for a basic tempo is imperative in most classically-conceived movements, for it is this that links the drama of events and gives the music its heart-beat and continuity. Like the human pulse the beat is not metronomic but flexible, and susceptible to changes of mood; but if it varies too much, or goes in fits and starts, the organism becomes ill. There is no room for fatigue in the *Waldstein*: it is as healthy and strong in its quietest moments as in its most exultant climaxes.

The opening *allegro con brio* inherited certain unusual features of key-behaviour from Op. 31, no. 1, but there the likeness stops. No earlier sonata had characterized its main subjects so strongly, and the wider contrast of key (E major instead of G major for the second group) enhances the mood-contrast between the rhythmic, pulsating first subject and the chorale-like E major theme. Two brief answering figures emerge from the former, and as they play a great part in the development they may as well be quoted:

C   33

EX. 9

The first subject grows rapidly but soon comes to a halt in C minor, as though meeting an impassable cliff-face. It makes a new start in the reverse harmonic direction, which accounts for the unorthodox orientation of the second group, the mediant replacing the dominant. Later in the movement, when the 'cliff-face' is encountered for the second time, the music takes evasive action and makes a delightful detour. Such surprises, like the famous 'wrong note' in the Schumann Piano Concerto, add zest to a recapitulation, and one other must be mentioned; the second subject, having first appeared in E major, understandably believes A major to be the correct key for its return. Here, as E. M. Forster's Helen would have said, Beethoven appears in person and turns a rather drastic modulation in mid-theme into an effect of pure poetry:

EX. 10

It is in the development section that Beethoven's new reserves of strength triumph. Having built up a page of sequences out of Ex. 9 he then turns to the second group, picks up the flowing sequel to the quasi-chorale theme, and takes it on a further

34

exploration of keys. This new juxtaposition of hitherto unrelated ideas is as dramatic as the exploration itself. New keys, however, may unlock familiar doors, and when C minor is reached in this context the significance is realized: its dominant can resolve equally well into the home key of C major, which it does through an exciting crescendo that resembles, without harmonically paralleling, the Fourth Symphony at this point. The coda is on the same grand scale, beginning with an alarming interruption that presents the first subject in D flat. Such moves, common in Beethoven, give an added freshness to the final peroration, in which elements of both subjects are aligned and, as it were, brought home.

Such a movement is as much a drama of keys as of themes, and no verbal analysis can do justice to the sweeping majesty of the writing or the sense of fulfilment in the C major-ness of the ending. Although the thematic relationships between movements were subtle, if they can be traced at all, the need for organizing moods and keys was obvious; and since the rondo of the *Waldstein* was to enjoy long stretches of C major harmony from the start a greater foil was required than the rather mild *Andante favori*. The replacement was ideal: a mysterious *adagio molto* fraught with ambiguous questionings and silences. These resolve into a short cantilena beginning in the rich 'cello register of the piano, after which the silences are filled in and explained, and the questionings lead insistently towards the home key of the sonata. Having achieved their goal they fade away and leave the final answer to the hushed, serene theme of the rondo. This theme, which cost Beethoven much pains in the making (see Ex. 13 on p. 39), is anchored to a deep pedal-note. It is important to keep this note sounding, even on a modern piano and at the risk of blurring the harmonies: the whole point of the passage is its mistiness, and full daylight does not arrive until the first fortissimo, which may have given the sonata its earlier nickname, 'L'Aurore'. The ease with which the rondo-theme spreads and repeats itself gives an early clue to the spacious layout, which allows for two stormy episodes in minor keys and a good deal of development besides. Has the very leisurely tempo-mark, *allegretto moderato*, an ulterior purpose? It has: for towards the end, after a great climax and a pause, Beethoven sets the rondo-theme spinning at more than double-quick time in a brilliant, triumphant *prestissimo*.

Sonata in F, Op. 54

Op. 54 has never been very popular: ironically enough, this is not because it is at all ordinary or conventional, but on account of its extraordinary unconventionality. It makes no attempt to scale heights or plumb depths like its neighbours, but exploits its own brand of detached humour. There are only two movements. The first, in minuet tempo, is twice interrupted by athletic double-octave passages in the manner of a study. The second is a toccata in unbroken semiquaver patterns that run in and out of remote keys with gentle but irrepressible initiative, giving extra prominence to its sonata-form development, and making its nearest rival, the finale of Op. 26, seem tame by comparison.

Sonata in F minor, Op. 57 (*Appassionata*)

Even Schindler, who wrote effusive accounts of Beethoven's free manner of playing, said of the later sonatas, in which he included the *Appassionata*, that they should be played in strict time 'for they permit few if any deviations and certainly do not demand them'. The *Appassionata*, like the *Waldstein*, has suffered from its own universal appeal: it is a challenge to the virtuoso, it fires the imagination of the poet, and appeals equally to the scholars and philosophers among pianists. The title added by the publisher is for once highly appropriate: it does not 'predispose our imaginations', like Czerny's description of ocean waves on a stormy night and a distant cry for help, though Beethoven occasionally did give such verbal interpretations informally. Let us, however, keep to the facts of the text. The first *allegro assai* is in twelve-eight time, and both main themes share the same rhythmic characterization:

EX. 11

36

The first sketches were in common time, and when Beethoven changed to twelve-eight he had to choose between quavers and semiquavers for the small notes of Ex. 11. He chose semiquavers, despite the more complex notation of ties, both for their increased tension and their unifying effect, and players who relapse into quavers lose a great deal of the music's character and drive. Driving force means not excessive speed, but steady propulsion, and it was the insistence of a triplet-rhythm that led the composer to abandon the original notation. This rhythm is first heard as a four-note figure in the bass – since it invariably appears on the same notes, three D flats falling to C, it has been associated with 'fate' – but it develops into an almost constant drumming as the movement proceeds and underpins the recapitulation of the opening bars.

There is no exposition repeat – a tradition, not always observed by performers anyway, which stemmed from the desire to give the listener a second chance of assimilating the material. Of the two possible reasons, one is that the urgent drama forbade any such formality; secondly, the exposition closes with a stormy paragraph in A flat *minor*, which leads more readily to new keys than old ones – in this case, enharmonically to E major. Otherwise sonata-form is carried through logically and relentlessly, with a climactic coda and a shattering *più allegro* finish. Throughout, dynamics are used far more explosively than in the *Waldstein* – as befits the nature of the work, which is tragic and dramatic where the other was exultant – and as for the frequent insistence on the Neapolitan sixth and the diminished seventh chords, Beethoven himself remarked that the serious composer still depended on the 'judicious use' of these tools-of-the-trade. (The Neapolitan sixth, a technical term, referred to the flattening of the second and sixth notes of the scale and the harmony deriving from these notes. Anyone who plays the piano a little will sense the emotional difference if the simple progression D–B–C is changed to D flat–B–C: D flat is the favourite 'Neapolitan' note of the *Appassionata* – pathetic or menacing, according to the way it is struck.)

Between the two storms of the *Appassionata* comes the peaceful *andante* with its variations. A great pianist of the romantic tradition exaggerated the contrast and said that the *andante* could not be played too slowly, nor the finale too fast. Beethoven indicated differently: he added *con moto* to the former and *ma non troppo* to

37

the *allegro*, for the clear reasons that the *andante* must have enough life to engender its flowing variations, while the finale must be held in check, so as not to forestall the whirlwind of its final *presto*. The theme of the *andante*, each half repeated, is as much harmonic as melodic and lies in a solemn low register; and the first three variations evolve by the old process of 'division', crotchet-movement giving way to quavers, semiquavers, and demisemiquavers. They also ascend by octaves and generate a climax, which collapses quickly into the final variation, a restatement of the theme, now distributed antiphonally between different registers. Its last chord is the famous 'interrupted cadence': our old friend the diminished seventh used with awe-inspiring effect, first pianissimo, then fortissimo – which should be played as at (*a*), with the 'secco' right-hand chord dramatically crowning the spread one in the left, not as at (*b*), as most of the older editions have it.

EX. 12

On this the torrent of the finale breaks in, a sonata-form movement largely derived from a subdued *moto perpetuo* subject, and, like the last movements of the *Moonlight* and the D minor sonatas, pursuing a single mood from start to finish. Here Beethoven asked for the latter part, not the exposition, to be repeated – which adds greatly to the cumulative effect of the whole and increases, by delaying it, the dramatic force of the *presto* coda.

INTERLUDE

OP. 78 TO OP. 81A

The *Waldstein* and the *Appassionata* having, in their different ways, carried the piano sonata to a climax, Beethoven gave the form a rest. The latter has, however, been ascribed by some writers to 1806, but sketches for it were well advanced by 1804 and its delayed publication seems most likely due to the composer's lack of a good copyist familiar with his handwriting, and to his absorption in other projects: *Fidelio*, the three middle symphonies, the *Razumovsky* quartets, the Mass in C, the Violin Concerto, and the G major Piano Concerto. If Beethoven in fact worked so slowly and laboriously we may well ask how he achieved so much, but his motto appears to have been 'always have plenty on hand' and if one composition gave him trouble he took up the threads of another, so that different works grew up simultaneously. They betray certain cross-influences too: the four-note *Appassionata* motive has an obvious relationship with the first movements of the Fifth Symphony and the G major Concerto, despite the latter's vast difference in character; and it is an interesting revelation of key-sensitivity that when both these works appear to 'quote' the figure verbatim at the beginnings of the development sections they should do so in the *Appassionata* key of F minor.

The work of Nottebohm and his successors on the sketches has far more than academic value. Their difficult task has been to track down the sketch-books, many of which were auctioned, dispersed and lost at the time of Beethoven's death, to decipher them, and to link and explain their loose threads. Moreover, the jottings were made only for the composer's own use, with no concessions to legibility, and sketches for a single work would often extend over years: the *allegro* theme of Op. 111, for instance, can be traced back twenty years to a phrase noted down in 1801 and marked *andante*. Nottebohm, in his analyses of Beethoven's composing methods, drew attention to two opposite procedures, which we might call 'sculptural' and 'architectural'. In some cases he would wrestle with a single theme, hammering away until it took its ultimate decisive shape. The rondo-theme of the *Waldstein* came into being in just this way:

EX. 13

39

(*continued*)

Here even the first two bars were elusive, yet their final pattern (*d*) – the bass C and the repeated treble G – was to determine the character of more than half the movement, a simple enough rhythmic germ, *once discovered*. On other occasions Beethoven dispensed with details and became an architect in sound, laying a kind of ground plan for an entire movement on a single stave, marking the modulations, and leaving blanks where the themes were not yet clear to him. (The *Eroica* is a famous example of the second group being born *out* of a movement in this way.) So, on the one hand, fragments might be worked out separately and then brought together; on the other, they might develop within the general conception – and naturally, as Nottebohm observed, many sketches hover between these extremes. But the sketches have a practical value for performers, too. They show, in the *Appassionata*, the trouble Beethoven took over notation; they show, in the coda of the *Waldstein* first movement, that the sudden pauses were introduced for a dramatic purpose—the abrupt withholding of the key-note—and suggest that they should be played with a sense of drama. The significance of a composer's second thoughts is often brought home vividly when we know his first thoughts. Nobody will hear or play the marvellous ending of Bach's E flat minor prelude (in the first book of the '48') in quite the same way after seeing the earlier unextended version; and the character of the opening theme in the Op. 90 Sonata seems all the more vivid when we know of the humdrum sequences that gave Beethoven the idea.

Sonata in F sharp, Op. 78
Sonata in G, Op. 79

When Beethoven returned to the piano sonata he eschewed the grand manner for a while (just as Brahms, many years later, turned to 'Intermezzi' after his symphonic triumphs, regarding the piano as a confidant), and although he simultaneously wrote down that strange improvisatory *Fantasia*, Op. 77, the next two sonatas are brief and concise. The F sharp major, Op. 78, was one of Beethoven's own favourites, perhaps because its intimate manner led others to underrate it, and partly no doubt because of its dedication to Therese von Brunswick, the 'dear beloved Therese' who gave him her portrait and inscribed it 'to the unique genius'. There are two movements only, and the four bars of *adagio* introduction to the first illustrate both the modest scale and the intimate, concentrated expression – a very different story from the early childlike two-movement sonatas of Op. 49, and one that looks forward at times to the distilled emotion of the late works. Here are a few bars from the coda of this movement, where the fragmentation of the first subject's upbeat and the contrapuntal writing in the left hand quite clearly presage the manner of the last quartets:

EX. 14

The second movement, an *allegro vivace*, is a hybrid in form, though it seems like a sonata-rondo. There are but two basic ideas, both capricious and epigrammatic, and they were summed up well, if irreverently, by the young pianist who announced them to an informal audience as 'First, "Rule, Britannia"; then, all in *twos*!'

A child might more easily respond to the direct emotions of the next sonata, Op. 79 in G, sometimes called 'sonatina'; but if the manner seems simple and sequential in all three movements this is because it is as completely impersonal as the previous work had been personal: it is certainly not an early work served up late by accident, and the development of the opening *presto alla tedesca* wrestles with the three crotchets of the theme in typical middle-period fashion.

D   41

Sonata in E flat, Op. 81a (Das Lebewohl)

A more personal note, this time in the grand manner, returns in the remaining sonata of 1809: Op. 81a in E flat, to which Beethoven himself gave a title, *Das Lebewohl*, and even spelt the word out in syllables over the first notes of the piece:

EX. 15

Although Beethoven was to relinquish the piano again for some years the 'farewell' of the title did not refer to that instrument but to one of his closest friends, the Archduke Rudolph, to whom he dedicated many of his most imposing works, including the so-called *Emperor* Concerto, the *Missa Solemnis*, and the B flat Trio, hence known as the *Archduke* Trio. It was no permanent farewell, but concerned Rudolph's temporary exile from Vienna during the Napoleonic bombardment; and the Sonata strikes no tragic or warlike note, being content to depict the normal friendly emotions of parting, absence and return – which are in fact the subtitles of the three movements. The common French title, *Les Adieux*, would have been anathema to Beethoven, all the same: he even rejected Italian terms as Napoleonic in his next two sonatas, and although he restored them from Op. 106 onwards he still described that work as for the *Hammerklavier*, the German equivalent of 'pianoforte'. The *Lebewohl* Sonata keeps to Italian tempo-marks, and prefaces the first movement with sixteen bars of *adagio*, beginning with the three-note motive of Ex. 15 – the simplest of horn-calls – and soon reharmonizing it with a chromatic twist towards the unlikely key of C flat. Those who wish to read more into the programme can find unrest and pathos in the continually shifting tonality, but the very word 'farewell' implies optimism rather than despondence, and no sooner is an optimistic note touched, almost accidentally, than it is taken up vigorously and cheerfully by the succeeding *allegro*. It may be noted that it is taken up on subdominant and not tonic harmony, which lends a special point to the recapitulation. Whether or not the *allegro* was intended to depict the brisk departure and safe journeying of the Archduke's coach is a matter for the listener's imagination, but there is an obvious sense of something receding into the distance in the poetic coda. The constant allusions to the *Lebewohl* theme, and its integration into the actual subjects of the *allegro*, foreshadow the technique of the *Leitmotiv*.

Beethoven expressed his thoughts on programme-music when he called the *Pastoral* Symphony 'more feeling than painting', and there is nothing to be gained by trying to read 'events' into the rest of the *Lebewohl* Sonata. Absence and reunion, however, imply sad and joyful emotions respectively, and composers have long turned to minor and major keys to express them. Unstable minor tonality may express not only pathos but disquiet, and in Beethoven's 'absence' movement the music, whether we associate tangible emotions with it or not, conveys just this restlessness. The form is unusual: it exposes a chain of ideas that immediately recapitulates itself in a different cycle of keys. But a third statement has no sooner begun than it drifts on to the dominant seventh of E flat and, recognizing this as a homecoming of souls as well as of tonality, the finale breaks in. The finale of the *Emperor* Concerto also breaks in on *its* slow movement, and, as the Sonata shares the same key, the same six-eight rhythm, the same year and, incidentally, the same dedicatee, it is not surprising to find similar keyboard patterns turning up – not in the theme, but in the passage-work. Both Sonata and Concerto took advantage of a still further extension of the keyboard. The *Lebewohl* finale is in sonata form, with a development section that disappoints its ambitions and soon gives way to the recapitulation; and there is a reflective treatment of the first subject in the *poco andante* coda; but the sonata as a whole does not quite live up to its noblest moments, sitting on the fence between middle-period brilliance and late-period introspection. The programme may be pleaded as an excuse; the sonata is a 'pièce d'occasion'. But the next sonata, Op. 90, is also supposed to have been inspired by an 'occasion' – which, however, we need not take too seriously; the music, in a much quieter way, is self-sufficient.

43

THE LAST SONATAS

OP. 90 TO OP. 111

Sonata in E minor, Op. 90

Another five years had elapsed, and the Op. 90 Sonata of 1814 has more claim to kinship with the great sonatas of the last period than to the previous ones. Its modesty is deceptive. But the minor-major contrast of two movements appealed to Beethoven, and he was to exploit it to the full in the last sonata of all, Op. 111. The explanation he gave of Op. 90 to Count Moritz von Lichnowsky, to whom it is dedicated, is amusingly mundane. The Count, who was about to marry a lady beneath his social station, was offered 'a struggle between the heart and the head' in E minor, followed by its resolution, a song-like sonata-rondo in E major: 'conversation with the beloved'. Hans von Bülow aptly epitomized the contrast as speech and song; others have suggested prose and poetry. The opening subject of the first movement was fashioned from an unpromising sketch of mechanical sequences, given significance by subtle moulding and dynamic gradations; and the key of E minor is only clinched in its lyrical continuation, the 'heart' of the conflict, a theme that later ends the movement without so much as an additional chord or *ritardando*. The development section, often cited for its economy, derives entirely from the rhythmic and melodic elements of the first subject: the 'head' is at work. As for the second movement, Mendelssohn, who admired this sonata, would have been proud to claim it as a 'song without words'; yet once again the sketches show that the impression of unhurried ease was not achieved at once – the phrases of the song required skilful dovetailing. The episodes, all closely related, are involved in the general mood, and after the rondo-theme has sung its way for the fourth time, in a new rich tenor register, there is a moment of tender retrospect and the most delicate of all sonata endings. This music does far more than evoke a serene tranquil mood: it is a distillation of thought and emotion, and there is a renewed interest in the expressive powers of counterpoint in the coda – which brings us into the world of the last five sonatas.

44

Sonata in A, Op. 101

The closing bars of Op. 90 are hard enough to put across in the concert hall: Beethoven has written a *ritardando* over the dying phrases of the theme, and he now adds a *crescendo* and *accelerando* over a delicate passage of semiquavers that only reach the initial tempo halfway through the penultimate bar; he then adds a *subito pp* for the last bar of all. Such delicacy of expression cannot be inflated without losing the rapt, intimate mood. Solo sonatas were in fact seldom played in public in Beethoven's day; they were chamber music in the true sense, works for domestic sharing and enjoyment; and the radio listener today is often better off than his counterpart in the back row of the stalls – though this depends on the work being played. There are sonatas that storm the heights, like the *Appassionata* and the *Hammerklavier*, and there are others that confide, like Op. 90 and Op. 101. But the *Hammerklavier*, with the grandest scale of all, also confides, in its profoundly personal *adagio*; and Op. 101, on the threshold of the last period, follows each of its intimate movements with vigorously rhythmic ones. According to Schindler, this was the only piano sonata to have been publicly performed in Beethoven's lifetime, but the date – February 1816 – suggests, ironically, the still more intimate Op. 90, since the A major Sonata, Op. 101, was not completed until that summer. Beethoven wished the dedication to be a surprise, but it was artistic admiration rather than romantic attachment that led him to choose the Baroness Dorothea von Ertmann. She was a pianist who made up in expression for what she lacked in physical strength, renowned for her intuitive understanding of Beethoven's style, and he obviously had her in mind when he asked for the first movement to be played *mit der innigsten Empfindung*. This direction, 'with innermost feeling', was far subtler than the *viel Ausdruck* (much expression) of Op. 81a, and it comes again in the variations of Op. 109.

All the first movements of the late sonatas follow the sonata-form pattern, which was so instinctive to Beethoven that almost any line of thought could be channelled this way. But the variety of thought and the flexibility of the form, within its chosen bounds, are amazing – freedom within strictness, which is a far more potent artistic weapon than freedom uncontrolled. Yet the quiet opening of Op. 101 seems informal, as though one had entered the room in the middle of a conversation:

EX. 16

The tempo is moderate, and the continuous lyrical flow makes any analysis into subjects distasteful, though the usual phases of development and recapitulation are clear enough and the key-scheme is straightforward. It is in the unbroken line and the avoidance of full closes that we sense a new style: each cadence gives birth to the next phrase, opening up fresh vistas without disturbing the gentle, temperate climate. The climate, however, changes abruptly with the next movement, a lively *alla marcia* in the unexpected key of F major, the vitality being maintained, even in quiet passages, by an all-pervading dotted rhythm that is bandied about between the parts in string-quartet fashion. Here the form is binary, with repeats, though the second half has out-grown itself in the manner of some of Bach's preludes in the Second Book of the '48', and it hints at a recapitulation without committing itself to details, so that new shapes continue to emerge until three bars from the end. The trio section, always considered as a separate entity in such classical analyses, is in B flat: a strangely spare experiment in canonic writing, with quiet angular phrases shadowing and foreshadowing each other, sometimes at a bar's distance, sometimes in half-bars. It links up with the return of the march; and it also ties up with Beethoven's growing interest in counterpoint, which shows itself again in the fugal treatment of the finale theme and was to dominate all in the last movement of the next sonata, Op. 106.

Op. 101 continues with a slow movement, whose grave hushed atmosphere is enhanced by the continuous use of the soft pedal and the absence of such expressive devices as crescendos, diminuendos, fortes and pianos. It is like a whispered commentary on the great slow movement of the D major Cello Sonata, written the previous year; but its outcome is more nearly parallel to the D major's companion, the C major Cello Sonata, for it closes into a reminiscence of the opening of the whole work (Ex. 16) which

46

in turn leads, excitedly, into the finale. Such overt reminiscences became common with the later Romantics, but they were rare enough with Beethoven. In Op. 27, no. 1, he took a backward glance at the *adagio* in the coda of the finale. He called that sonata a fantasy, and (according to Schindler) he called the first and third movements of Op. 101 'impressions and reveries', all of which points to the personal nature of the music. The use of a short slow movement as a foil to the finale had been explored in the *Waldstein*, though not with such subjective mood-directions as *sehnsuchtsvoll* and *mit Entschlossenheit* – 'with yearning' and, for the finale, 'with resolution'. In Op. 101 there is no spacious rondo: the sonata ends with a bright movement in concentrated sonata-form, with a superbly cumulative fugal development. Even its playful moods show an intellectual delight in counterpoint, as in the later counterstatement of the 'resolute' first subject, which appears in the bass of Ex. 17:

EX. 17

Sonata in B flat, Op. 106 (Hammerklavier)

By 1819 the *Hammerklavier* was ready. It was the most titanic of all the sonatas, both in gestures and in time-scale, a triumphant enlargement of the four-movement plan to epic proportions; though it must be emphasized that the common title has no more than chauvinistic significance. The preceding years were comparatively unproductive, except of misery: the endless litigation over his adopted nephew Karl, bad health, no hope for his deafness, and money problems. His mind, however, was full of the most momentous projects, the *Missa Solemnis* and the Ninth Symphony, both of which took five or more years to come to fruition. The *Hammerklavier* was already on this scale. After the Ninth, Beethoven devoted himself to the string quartet; and after

47

the *Hammerklavier* the sonatas become more intimate again. Everest had first to be climbed. Tragic evidence of Beethoven's financial position was his readiness to compromise with a London publisher over the sonata's length by omitting whole movements – he had neither time nor inclination to write an alternative work – though there can have been very few prospective purchasers capable of tackling it in any form. When Weingartner, a century later, dispersed the technical difficulties by orchestrating the *Hammerklavier* he also destroyed its essential character: the sense of superhuman effort. The triumph of Everest would be nothing if one arrived at the summit by helicopter. The Sonata in B flat, Op. 106 – to give it its proper title – was dedicated to the Archduke Rudolph, and among the sketches for it there is a variant of the opening theme set to the words 'vivat, vivat Rudolphus', a birthday greeting for a four-part chorus, which gives a clue, if one were needed, to the vociferous start of the sonata itself:

EX. 18

This arresting opening is immediately balanced by a wonderfully lyrical phrase, and these dramatically opposed elements epitomize the wide emotional range of the movement. Paradoxically, large-scale music benefits from split-second moments of drama, and when Ex. 18 is restated after the first page it suddenly hammers on a chord of D major, thus unlocking the door to G major, in which the second group unfolds in long sweeping, overlapping paragraphs. The term 'group', instead of 'subject', was never more appropriate, for there are at least six ideas in this part of the exposition, including a haunting cantabile in long notes, that does in fact 'haunt' the otherwise busy development and coda. Its special emotional flavour results from an elusive mixture of major and minor tonality, E flats and B flats in G major. Mozart knew well how to throw shadows on a bright theme in this way, and in late Beethoven the mixture has an

48

introspective purport, a wistfulness of the spirit. We met it in the finale of Op. 101, where the minor ninth gave a bitter tang to a child-like repeating phrase (bar 21 et seq.); we find it less in the last sonatas of all, and most often in the still later quartets, to which the *Hammerklavier* looks forward in many ways, formally and spiritually. To return to the first movement, the imperious opening gesture provides ample material for an energetic fugue in the development, and the events at the double-bar before this starts show that will-power alone can establish new keys: Beethoven leaps and stays, with the briefest harmonic formalities – in fact, if the marked repeat is made, the chord of B flat is sufficient to make the *key* B flat.

The scherzo comes second: so does the Ninth Symphony's. In both instances the profound meditations of an *adagio* demanded postponement, but there the comparison stops. The Ninth magnified the traditional dance-movement, if we may regard the scherzo as a galvanizing of the steps of the minuet, into an unparalleled outburst of rhythmic energy. The scherzo of Op. 106 is a strangely whimsical affair, full of quirks: the scherzo-idea is a one-bar epigram that builds up phrases by self-repetition in sequences, and it is harmonized-out even to its dotted rhythm, as though in four moving parts – once again the quartet influence is at hand. Other harmonic tendencies are typical of the third-period style: the anticipating of resolutions, and the occasional modal flavour. The former dispelled the harmonic tyranny of the bar-line; the latter, which reached its climax in the 'Incarnatus' of the *Missa* and the 'Heiliger Dankgesang' of the Op. 132 Quartet, reflected Beethoven's growing love of Palestrina. The scherzo of Op. 106 hints at modal harmony in its darker phrases.

Musical analysts can have a field-day with the *Hammerklavier*, and may begin by observing that the 'Rudolphus' theme (Ex. 18) is marked by a rising and a falling third: B flat to D, D to B flat; and then note that this contour is discernible not only in the scherzo theme and its strange widely-spaced trio, but in the opening of the slow movement too, and maybe, with some mental ingenuity, in the final fugue. Whether by intent or instinct, the unity of the work is manifest without recourse to actual cross-quotation, as in Op. 101, but Beethoven satisfied the theorists when he felt the need to add a preliminary bar to the *adagio* as an afterthought, with an upward third matching the downward third of the theme:

EX. 19

This *adagio* being one of the greatest and also one of the longest single movements in classical piano music, any adequate analysis, or attempt to describe its details, would fill a whole chapter. Tovey, in his *Companion to Beethoven's Pianoforte Sonatas*, takes five pages. (His approach is intentionally technical, but this should not scare off anyone who has studied harmony and thinks it dull, for his digressions and side-commentaries, like those in his edition of the sonatas, are as humanly witty and revealing as anything in the English language.) The size of the *adagio* is in proportion to the breadth and number of its themes, which are unfolded in the fullest sonata-form and the fullest range of key-board eloquence to be found anywhere in the sonatas. It is interesting that its rare key of F sharp minor should also have inspired one of Mozart's profoundest slow movements, the *adagio* of the famous A major Concerto (K.488), and that both works should turn in their opening themes to stress the Neapolitan chord of G major: but where Mozart deepened the effect of pathos Beethoven expanded his into a brief glimpse of heaven, a different emotional use of a similar harmonic device. Although the opening mood suggests a lone, grave contemplation, the music encompasses considerable passion and profound tranquillity in turn, and since the first theme is the subject of the development it is disguised by elaborate decoration when it returns, leaving the simple form for the coda. But this is too summary a description: there is hardly an obvious or untended repetition in the movement.

The final fugue, to crown all sonata-fugues, is approached through a fantastic passage of recitative, in which a continual descent through the whole gamut of keys is interrupted from time to time for orientation. When the chord of A is reached for the second time, with conspicuous excitement, the harmony drops out and the bass falls quietly to F. Together F and A suggest the dominant of the home-key, B flat: this is the cue for the fugue to begin, a dramatic moment of 'recognition' which had been worked, far less elaborately, in the *Lebewohl* Sonata. The fugue of the *Hammerklavier* is as formidable a challenge to any player's technique and stamina as it was to Beethoven's hard-won mastery of counterpoint, and it used to be criticized on both counts. There are still two opposite schools of thought: some complain that a few of the later works strain the medium too much, whether that medium happens to be the chorus in the Ninth, the quartet in the *Grosse Fuge*, or the piano in the *Hammerklavier*, and maintain that the ultimate test of a composer is that he should be grateful to play. Others, the loyal Beethovenites, believe that where the musical thought is so lofty both performer and listener must strive to meet it. But nowadays the *Hammerklavier* fugue deters fewer and fewer virtuosos: the danger is that one day it may be made to sound easy. This it must not: the leaping trills and the jagged angles of the counterpoint, with its fierce augmentations and intellectual reversals of the subject, crabwise, are a mental as well as a physical battle. Out of it emerges, in the fugue, a tranquil D major section, which combines, marvellously, with the principal subject. And out of the triumph of the whole sonata there emerged the more accessible, less superhuman, Beethoven of the three remaining piano sonatas.

Sonata in E, Op. 109

Having worked the four-movement plan on the grandest scale in Op. 106, Beethoven achieved a new conciseness, a new flexibility, in the last sonatas of all. They bow to no conventional order of events, and the weight and distribution of the various sections is unique in each case. Op. 109 and Op. 111, for instance, end with slow movements in variation-form and fulfil themselves in moods of tranquillity that would have been shattered by the return-to-earth of an orthodox finale. But even these two 'comparable' movements are very different in approach, Op. 109 relying on the *contrast* of variations, Op. 111 on their gradual accumulation. The former carries its allegiance through to the re-emergence of the original theme, the latter takes wings in a long, transfigured coda. Op. 110 has the most unusual finale of all: a combination of recitative, aria, and fugue. Yet these works have been called a trilogy, and efforts have been made to interrelate their themes, a pastime that pays better dividends in the late quartets, where Beethoven himself pointed the way by

51

quoting the *Grosse Fuge* subject in Op. 132. Spiritual unity may manifest itself in common turns of phrase, and the arioso of Op. 110 achieves its *dolente* character with a downward minor scale strikingly similar to that used by Bach in 'Es ist vollbracht' in the *St John Passion*, a work Beethoven probably never knew. On the other hand the aspiring fugue-subject in the same movement seems to derive from the opening of the whole sonata. 'Seems to' is sufficient: the same mind, after all, created both. Any further links between the different sonatas can be attributed to the fact that they share a style and language. They were completed in 1820, 1821 and 1822 respectively: the only important products of those years, unless we include the overture *Zur Weihe des Hauses*, an 'occasional' piece full of jubilant Handelian counterpoint. Work on the *Missa* and the Ninth Symphony still continued. Each of the three sonatas, however, makes its own formal laws.

Op. 109 prefaces its spacious variation-finale with two short movements, both in sonata form. The first, in barely four minutes, establishes a dual character by the direct opposition of *vivace* and *adagio* themes, the latter interrupting the former almost at once. The sequence of keys is normal, the abrupt juxtaposition and the contrast of mood and manner are unusual: there is no transition – an interrupted cadence effects the change from first to second subject, typical of the movement's compression. Yet there is no sense of haste in the *vivace*: it is qualified *ma non troppo* and begins by unfolding an innocent diatonic theme, rather like a chorale, but in broken figuration. A diminished-seventh chord in this context is dramatic, still more so when it launches such an unexpected paragraph of rapturous, expressive improvisation. In the development the *vivace* returns and the fluttering figuration, worked out with the consistency of a Bach 'pattern' prelude, leads to the climax of the recapitulation and, matching the opening, to a further irruption of the *adagio*. The coda, in which the first idea melts into an inspired phrase of pure harmony, is in perfect proportion, with a touch of minor-major pathos in the closing bars. Beethoven had shown, in the Fourth Concerto, the strength of tenderness: he does so here, too. But, without a break, the second movement shatters the contemplative mood in a resolutely defiant E minor *prestissimo*, in six-eight time. The steps in the bass should be noticed, as they are developed as an independent theme later, thus giving a new meaning to the return of the opening. There is no trace of the traditional scherzo form: everything is compressed into a tense, terse sonata-form movement, a perfect foil to the variations that follow. The subject of these is one of Beethoven's most intimate and touching melodies, and the variations follow its binary shape with classical precision, though one or two generously vary the repeats still further. In brief, variation 1 superimposes its own eloquent melody upon the original harmonies, variation 2 alternates a light semiquaver outline with a rich stretto of counterpoints on the repeat of each half (a 'double' variation), while the third variation is in vigorous double counterpoint, like a Bach two-part invention. Variations 4 and 5 are also contrapuntal, the former warmly spacious and expressive, the latter again vigorous and fugal in texture; there is an abrupt change to the tempo and mood of the original in variation 6, which builds up a mountain of scales and trills out of a reiterated pedal-note; and when the theme re-emerges in its quiet simple form it appears ineffably enhanced in the light of all these adventures.

Sonata in A flat, Op. 110
Over the opening bars of the next sonata, Op. 110, are inscribed the words 'con amabilità', sufficient guide to the warmth of heart inherent in all the first-movement themes. It unfolds in an unhurried cantabile, and the one non-vocal idea, a transition arpeggio figure of the lightest, most delicate texture, shows its subservience to the first subject by playing around it in the recapitulation. Everything is in orderly and predictable sonata form, the short development dealing exclusively with the first subject, except that a magic enharmonic modulation turns the recapitulation to E major instead of the home key of A flat, a process Beethoven checks in the nick of time. (Those who find this sudden change of gear alarmingly incongruous should try the experiment of reading F flat major for E major in this 'enharmonic' section, a hideously complex notation Beethoven avoided using. It is a matter for the eye, not the ear, but it can affect the performer's whole approach to the passage.) In the coda, which flows inevitably and naturally out of the existing material, we see, once again, Beethoven turning to counterpoint as an apotheosis of melody, and it is in the alto part of the fourth bar quoted that some people hear a foreshadowing of the last-movement fugue:

53

EX. 20

The second movement is a terse scherzo-and-trio in two-four time, with antiphonal use of dynamics, F minor *piano* being at once answered with C major *forte*. Its quirks continue in the trio, where abrupt leaps are followed by perilous descents of quavers, and where the left hand, crossing over, tends to mask the right hand's subsequent leap – a matter of importance for the player to adjust. The return of the scherzo collapses on to a quiet major harmony that is resolved, darkly, at the start of the next movement.

The first movement of the *Hammerklavier* and the finale of Op. 101 had leant heavily on fugal treatment in their development sections, and the *Hammerklavier* finale explored the fugue, in its own right, to the uttermost. There were plenty of precedents for integrating fugal devices with sonata form, and the most astonishing had been in the finale of Mozart's *Jupiter* Symphony, where most of the themes exercised themselves in counterpoint en route, in preparation for the final *tour de force* of the coda. But in Op. 110, whose finale has no connexion with sonata form whatever, the fugue is called in for a subjective emotional reason, the gathering of confidence after illness or despair. (This is not too much to read into it, as the words 'ermattet' and 'wieder auflebend', written over the second arioso and second fugue, mean literally 'exhausted' and 'gaining new life'. And the convalescent *Dankgesang* of the Op. 132 Quartet was clearly a translation into music of a personal experience.) The form may be briefly outlined as follows: recitative, arioso dolente, fugue, second arioso, second fugue. The recitative gropes its way through remote keys before settling in A flat minor for the first plaintive arioso, from whose cadence the fugue-subject arises in the tonic major. The forward march of the fugue, with its boldly striding upward fourths, is checked on its (apparently) penultimate chord, which resolves unexpectedly into G minor, the arioso now running its course again in faltering accents, as though grief-stricken. But its final cadence brings a quiet major chord, nine times repeated with growing strength, and out of this cloud of sound the fugue-subject emerges in inverted form, at first tenta-tively. Through various complexities of diminutions and augmentations (now in its original 'direct' version) it finds its way back home to A flat, gathering momentum and confidence, and losing its contrapuntal texture and becoming purely melodic in the last triumphant bars. Once again the finale has carried more than half the weight of the Sonata.

Sonata in C minor, Op. 111

In Op. 111, the last of all, it might be said that the 'argument' is equally apportioned, for there are only two movements and they make their contrast on all possible levels: *allegro con brio ed appassionato* and *adagio molto semplice e cantabile*, sonata form and variation form, extreme turbulence and profound serenity, the material and the spiritual worlds, the minor and the major key. Was this then the ultimate solution to the unity of the sonata, the resolving in one movement of the problems of the other? The stage for the work is, however, set in a page of slow introduction that gives an impression of immense breadth within a few bars of *maestoso*, and makes the point that one way of emphasizing an eventual tonic key is to lead away from it in the early phases, a habit of Haydn's that Beethoven had turned to amazing account at the start of his Fourth Symphony. In Op. 111 three challenging phrases in a sharply dotted rhythm close into a quiet exploration of the remotest keys before settling on to a dominant pedal of C minor, and the music shows signs of extinguishing itself when a sudden crescendo launches the *allegro*, a movement easily analysable into sonata form though unique in its compression and content. The transition, for example, is neither a spacious bridge-passage with new material as in Op. 110, nor is it crystal-lized into a single interrupted cadence as in Op. 109: it is a stormy fugato arising straight out of the notes of the first subject–a fate-like motive derived and vitalized from an early sketch-book. The second group, too, is both concise and full of dramatic incident: its six bars of lyrical melody have a glorious sense of space. In the exposition they are violently interrupted, but in the recapitulation they find their own way back into the storm; and this, having reached its greatest climax, subsides quickly, with a strange lightening of the sky in its last phase.

Beethoven rejected many versions of the *adagio* theme, the Arietta, before achieving its simple, sublime ultimate shape. The falling intervals C–G and D–G of the first two bars were not in the original sketches, and it makes one wonder whether Beethoven absorbed these from his work on the Diabelli Variations. Variation form, like the fugue, was a severe mental discipline. But whereas the Op. 109 variations had each viewed the theme from a new angle, in Op. 111 they grow logically one from another, with subdivisions of increasing complexity. In this way the celestial calm of the theme yields to a mood of tremendous exaltation by the time the third variation is reached. This is followed by one which alternates dark bass colours with ethereally light passage-work in the treble, after which the strict variation procedure is abandoned for a time. The chain of trills that ascends into higher and higher regions of the keyboard is one of the most daringly inspired effects in all music, so daring that it used to be criticized for its very bareness. For many others, including Tovey, it was an 'ecstatic vision'. The remaining coda is sufficiently vast to encompass a complete apotheosis of the original theme, now with an extension of its cadence: there is a climax, dissolving into the most ethereal version of all, transfigured (once again) with trills, and the ending has the noblest simplicity.

After he had composed this sonata Beethoven expressed his dissatisfaction with the piano as a means of expression, forsaking it for continued work on the Ninth Symphony and the *Missa Solemnis* and, eventually, for the last string quartets. He returned to it for some Bagatelles and for the monumental Diabelli Variations. But Op. 111 remained, significantly, his last word on the piano sonata.